The LAWS *of* PRACTICE

The Art of Following the Steps to Greater Dimensions in Living!

Dr. Undrai Fizer

IVINE HOUS
B O O K S

ISBN: 979-889619291-6

TABLE OF CONTENTS

INTRODUCTION

Listen,
I began to Practice from the Manifestation
of my Desire "before I actually received,
experienced, and lived from that Desire!"
The Desire or Vision itself, presented "hints"
into my own Spirit of what its Desires
were also.

I "hit and missed" for years UNTIL I actually
caught what it desired from Me! The Vision
and Myself "BOTH" wanted something
significant from the other; LIFE!

If YOU are desiring something Significant,
but with bare, average effort, STOP NOW!
You don't want it. You're just drawn to the
"bells and whistles!"

But if you're serious, YOU already know
what I'm speaking of.

Go Get it!
"Coach"

CHAPTER 1
Aiming For The Goal?

RESULTS are Manifestations, produced by a SEED called EFFORT. EFFORT is an Action provided by the FOLLOWER of a thing. INSTRUCTIONS are the STEPS to a SPECIFIC Ending or Result.

How I "FOLLOW THE STEPS" will determine the nature of the Outcome that I reveal. I can either follow the Instructions adamantly and with intention. Or, I can casually follow the Steps with procrastination, lack of depth and commitment, or even skip specific steps of the Instruction and produce absolutely NOTHING but excuses.

The Price YOU pay, nor the Instructions themselves, are responsible for NOTHING. **It is your following and commitment to the Steps, that determine what YOU receive. The Money does nothing.**

Sometimes, we desire to pay cheap prices, **simply because we are making a way for a cheap effort.** We know that we will not practice the methods to the degree of the high investment. We pay cheap in order to practice cheap. Paying a high value, for low value effort, is a loss of investment. We pay low, **in order to do "low!"**

Many will respond with, "Man, that cost too much," not because of the Product, but because we know that we have not been impacted in the Product to the point that our efforts will match the Significance of the Product.

Many simply desire to invest to the degree of their own return of effort. **HIGH NATURE PURPOSES will intimidate "low effort" individuals.** This is how we recognize our audience.

Yes, the masses need the HIGH NATURE PRODUCT. But have you recognized the posture of their efforts? *How do they respond to your calls? How do they communicate? Do their actions leave you in a state of confusion? Do they speak clearly and assertive? What's their follow-through like? Are they constantly late? Are they taking full responsibility for their actions? What are they passionate about? How is their patience level? Do you trust them? Or, are you constantly making excuses to continue on with them?*

Results manifest the degree of YOUR OWN EFFORTS and ADHERENCES. They are not a manifestation of your knowledge. They reveal the capacity of your follow-ship of Instruction. Even skipped steps produce a non-designed product. If I follow instructions in a wealthy fashion, I will receive the Wealth of the Product. If I follow the instruction inconsistently, absent of passion, lacking effort, I will receive the least of that Product.

CHAPTER 2
Maximum Effort!

Many will blame the cost of a Product and not their follow-through capacity within themselves. Many desire to pay a Price for a Product to produce itself on its own merit. *"If I pay $100 dollars to learn how to write a book, I want the book to write itself!"* We refuse to practice writing in a certain space of time. We don't take the time to practice, and evict other areas of *life-ing* from our space. We are up and down in our commitment to stick with the plan. And after awhile, we feel like we were cheated out of $100 dollars. But the truth is this, ***WE CHEATED OURSELVES out of follow-through.***

The KINGDOM is a result of **a Self, follow-through.** WE are either producing KINGDOMS, or cycles of Poverty and Lack. It is our own practices of Instructions that produce *"the whats and hows" of our lifestyle expression.* **My practices must match or transcend, the price of the Greatness I desire.** Greatness is not a mere word to throw around like a cliché. **It is the reality of my EFFORTS. It is the nature of the EFFORT I provide towards my Passion. My Practice determines my PURPOSE**.

My FUTURE is hidden within my Following of Instructions. It is not in how much money I paid to learn. It is in the Practice of what I am instructed. **If I don't trust my own consistency, I will sabotage the investments I have made.** If I invest $2 dollars for a thing that cost $1000, I am not saying that I cannot afford the full value of what I am pursuing. *I am saying that My efforts in commitment are worth $2 dollars.*

If I pay a thousand dollars into a thing, my effort must be worth more than a thousand to manifest the Intensity of the Purpose. Our lack of effort *"cheapens and devalues the cost of the thing,"* for the sake of destroying the demands of responsibility that the thing requires of us.

If I desire to escape, or defund the value of the thing, I must remove its requirements from my life by not subjecting my efforts to what it is asking me to do.

KINGDOMS are manifestations of ROYAL EFFORTS. Slums are manifestations of enslaved efforts, or the need of someone else doing things for me. **If I need to become the recipient of someone else's loyalty and commitment, then I will sit back, and do absolutely NOTHING**. My lack of effort, is a result of the Poverty I have allowed myself to thrive in. The

Instructions or Steps to GREATNESS, have been provided. If I choose not to follow the Instructions to the degree of the Instructor, what were my reasons for not doing so? *If GREATNESS is given in a map, then what are the reasons that I AM STILL LOST?*

Cheap-effort individuals may actually know that they are "cheap-effort" individuals. They become offended by high-effort people. They are easily offended with ROYAL Practitioners of Purpose. They will sabotage the Process and demand a refund. We all pay and follow-through, according to our degree to Practice.

When a naturally dis-interested person sees a Product that excites them, they naturally promise to give up everything and pay for the product. But after a few payments, their natural pattern rises again, and they suddenly become angered by the commitment that they once promised themselves. They now perceive their commitment as an evil force in their lives, and they will do whatever they can in order to get the Product to *"quit and leave their presence!"*

CHAPTER 3
Determine The Impact Of The Goal

Your truest desire to live the Result, will determine the Nature of the Effort you provide. To live the Result is to create the Result by how YOU actually live the Steps to the thing. If you desire the Result, while lacking the effort, your heart is actually a "thief," and the Journey will place a warrant for your arrest. The Atmosphere that resonates around the Result you "desire," will render YOU *as an unworthy pursuer!*

Desiring, what YOU refuse to practice for, follow instructions for, is ROBBERY! Covetousness is a crime. It is to create ways for someone else to either lose, or give up their own treasures for free. It is a form of manipulation in order to flatter them out of their own worth.

QUESTION:

Is your follow-thru, ROYAL? Do you follow Instructions to the degree that the Instructions inquire, in order to experience *"the cake shown on the box?"* Cheap deposits do not enable RICH RESULTS! A cheap follow-thru, WILL NOT PRODUCE a WEALTHY OUTCOME! A lazy practice WILL NOT PRODUCE a DIVINE NATURE! **Intentions do not create anything.**

Follow-thru, does!

Excuses only provide us with a second chance to mess it up again. Excuses produce nothing but "new opportunities" to remain in the past!

Even teaching those who refuse to follow the Instructions to the Degree they are designed to be followed, can cause the Teacher *to devalue the pearls that they are giving out. Even Jesus said to protect the value of your Treasures, and not to give them to "the swine!"* The swine is a mindset that will eat everything from every source. They do not recognize the differences of value between eloquent cuisine nor slop.

CHAPTER 4
Discern Where To Invest Your Time

Invest your treasures into Great Practitioners! YOU WILL ALL REAP A HARVEST!

Great Results do not create themselves. They will require your true adherence to the STEPS. They require YOU to do what they say, in all seasons. And not to your Convenience. **RESULTS do not grant Grace to your inconveniences nor excuses**. RESULTS are *"laws that worked hard and responsibly for the success it is now experiencing for itself!"*

Have YOU ever considered that? Have YOU ever considered that RESULTS ARE LAWS that have already received its success and legitimacy for what is has ALREADY PERFORMED AND MANIIFESTED?

The GREATNESS of the RESULTS is determined by the GREATEST EFFORTS AND PRACTICES from the PRACTIONER! Greatness is not a simple verbiage to be thrown about. PRACTICE and FOLLOW-THRU are the crowning jewels of the Practitioner. **WE ARE, what WE RECEIVE, from HOW WE DO!**

If I lackadaisically, or commonly/casually

exercise an Instruction, I will receive my own degree of effort back to Me. I receive what I invest in Me. **I do not receive what I pay for. I receive what I practiced for.** I receive the return of my follow-thru. I receive the essence of my own seed, back to Me. Nothing reaps nothing. **If I do not believe in ME, I will not do for ME. I may pay money for ME, but I will not perform for ME. I will seek for my monies to give it to ME. I may pay for a soda, and get it out of the refrigerator. BUT IT REQUIRES WORK FOR ME TO MAKE THE PRODUCT MYSELF!**

Many seek to buy WISDOM for a fee. Many seek to buy DELIVERANCE for a fee. DELIVERANCE FROM POVERTY cannot be found in a book. The Instructions to FREEDOM may be written in pages. BUT THE RESULTS ARE FOUND IN YOUR OWN HANDS, EFFORTS, and ADHERENCES TO WHAT IS WRITTEN IN THE PAGES! The Books do nothing without your Practices. Just because YOU CAN READ THE INFORMATION, QUOTE THE INFO, and WRITE DOWN THE INFO, means absolutely nothing. *Being lazy, with Powerful Things, will leave you a prisoner to generational limitations.*

PRACTICE and Following Instructions, are the prices WE PAY towards the

INFORMATION we purchased. We pay for the Instructions with money. Then, we pay for what we purchased with money, with **MUSCLE, MENTAL, and DISCIPLINE.** What we've purchased with money, requires our EFFORTS to reveal the reasons we read the information. The greater the fee, the greater the effort! We make valuable things "cheap" because of our cheap efforts. Or, we can make expensive things POWERFUL, when we grace the fee with expensive EFFORT and FOLLOW-THRU!

A procrastinator desires to "rest his/her effort" while making the Information "do the work and fight the battles!" They want to save energy, "while forcing the RESULTS to exhaust its energy," for the sake of providing for them.

We win because of ourselves. We lose because of ourselves. The KINGDOM, or the slums, are within OUR OWN HANDS!

CHAPTER 5
We Are What We Do!

Our practices, follow-throughs, and adherences, are direct reflections of how we practice our own lives. If we feel we are "cheap images," we will dare not invest in *"high maintenance methods!"* We will seek to pay for how we perceive ourselves. *We will seek "cheap knock offs" of the original.* We will seek *"high maintenance" information "facilitated by low achieving mentalities and dreamers!"* We will feel intimidated by Masters, yet encouraged by liars. We will seek seminars with cheap costs, who only require attendance for the videos and photo ops! We sow into what our efforts require of us.

When we perceive our DIVINE ROYALTY and NATURE, we seek and pursue Demands that will provoke our Greatest Degree of Imagination, Creativity, and RESPONSE TO ABILITY! We place ourselves in situations that motivate our Greatest Degree of FOLLOWING INSTRUCTIONS, DIRECTIONS, and DESTINY! We receive in return, the nature of our PRACTICES!

WE find ourselves actually "living up to the degree of WHO WE SENSE WE ARE," and our practices and methods AFFIRM and CONFIRM our identity. Who we feel that GOD *"says that we are,"* are revealed through how we follow directions and instructions! If we follow directions casually, we are but an "insignificant piece of GOD's creative design!" We sense that we are nothing. *OUR NEEDS ARE MORE HUNGRIER THAN OURSELVES. Our LACK STARVES more than our own Beliefs!*

But when we follow directions with POWER, we are the POWER of the CREATION. WE are the majestic ones who have discovered that they are *"favorites" with GOD, and a "Sharer of the DIVINE REALITY"* with HIM. We PRACTICE WHAT WE PAY FOR. WE FOLLOW INSTRUCTIONS to the LEARNING and DISCOVERIES we desire to EXPERIENCE.

I cannot afford to wait on what my desires and inner yearning are hungry to SEE. If we are connected to things that can hold off VISION, then the Hunger will not arrest our FOLLOW-THRU! If my SEASONS are pre-occupied with BUSY-ness, My Practices will wane in despair. I will not be in a HURRY to produce a thing that is deemed in the category of "EVENTUALLY, I'd like to SEE…"

If I can "wait to see it," I will not feel adamant to practice it. If I have other things to do, I will not be in a rush to perform it. Follow-through will not be considered an emergency to my Life. *If I don't need it now, it will not demand of Me, NOW!*

Our "FOLLOW-THROUGH" is determined by our need to "SEE IT! If we are not yearning to SEE IT, we will not be EMPOWERED TO PRACTICE IT! Our investments will be placed on HOLD. What we sow, will go into PAUSE!

My Vision provoked Me to practice it, WAY BEFORE I RECEIVED IT! I began to FOLLOW-THROUGH on my Instructions 'from the Future,' from Wisdom responsibilities that were placed in my CURRENT CONDITION! The "TOMORROW" I desired, required my OBEDIENCE within my TODAY! I could not afford to put off my *DIRECTION FOLLOWING* ATTRIBUTES! The LEGACY you seek is not in the passing down of money to your children, but within the AWAKENING of your children's ability to ***OBEY THE RULES OF POWER!***

When we receive the Benefits of our Parent's Practices and Adherences to the LAWS OF RESULTS, while not practicing those rules for ourselves, *we will create a POORHOUSE with the treasures from a WEALTHY HOUSE!* When we provide FAVOR to a Person who refuses to PRACTICE, we have just destroyed their lives "in the midst of beautiful things!"

CHAPTER 6
Discern Your Ways

HOW WE FOLLOW, as well as WHEN WE FOLLOW Directions, determine everything. GOD never blesses what we hear alone, but the degree in which we implement what is heard. GOD never blesses our attendance in a place, *but how we practice what is received and taken away, by our attendance in the Atmosphere.* Practice what YOU HAVE RECEIVED IN THE PRESENCE OF THE GREATER. If I seek to gain access for "cheap," PRACTICE what you have received by way of discount, *WITH YOUR WHOLE LIFE!* If someone grants mercy upon YOU, and allow YOU a "space at the Masters Table," begin to honor the Wealth of the Master by **"FOLLOWING DIRECTIONS" as though you invested FULL VALUE!** Honor the Hand of the GRACE GIVER, by paying for the "free" access to the Table of GODS "with your entire Life!" Don't simply gain access to tell others "in the hood" that YOU sat at the "celebrity table!" All you will gain of it is a mention, and a photo. *Yet, your house will be absent of POWER and MIGHT!*

How we value our Lives, will determine how we follow the Instructions to POWER, PURPOSE, and PROSPERITY! The Lives we say we desire, are not hidden in our Prayers alone, but within the Practices we exercise from the Directives we receive from Prayer and Investments. **We pay for what we purchased, through the Practices inspired from the Purchase! Without Practice, all we've done is spend money for nothing.** It's as though there was a hole in our pockets, and the money simply fell through!

If you are too tired to live as YOU, you will also be too tired to PRACTICE for the Life that is BEYOND yours! Purpose requires more than our understanding of the Rules, it also requires our FULL COMMITMENT of the Rules of the LIFESTYLE it produces. YOU must remember that you're creating a NEW LIFE, and not merely coloring "in a coloring book!"

If YOU invest in a Teacher, imitate their FAITH, RESILIENCE, and PRACTICE, by way of the RESULTS they authentically reveal from their lives; HEBREWS 13:7. PRACTICE AND IMITATE the GREATEST PRACTIONERS!

Your Way IS NOT enough. Your WAYS got YOU where YOU ARE, NOW. Your WAYS are requiring transformation and *not a mere tweaking!*

CHAPTER 7
Practice Winning Patterns

POVERTY is a manifestation of "self-anger," produced by SINCERE IGNORANCE. It's not just about MONEY. It's about ending up in LACK, after thinking YOU DID SOMETHING RIGHT! When we perceive that we can *SHORTCUT on the FULLNESS OF A REQUIREMENT,* the desired RESULT **"evicts its full portion" from the equation.** We cannot afford to "short cut" our Practices and expect a FULL PORTION! C'mon with that!

FOLLOW THROUGH is a DIVINE PRACTICE. Jesus said, *"I ONLY DO WHAT I SEE MY FATHER, SOURCE, VISION, DESTINY, doing!"* Jesus manifested through His Life, the RESULTS of FOLLOIWING DIRECTIONS, and PRACTICING the SPIRIT within His Father. He did more than hear and talk. HE WALKED "the Walk!" He exercised the METHOD! **Only the cheap doer, is offended with MASTER METHODS!** It's like a person who has nothing, while in the presence of the person with Something, saying to themselves, *"IT DON'T TAKE ALL OF THAT!"* That is why that person has NOTHING!

Jesus found pleasure in **PRACTICING GOD!** The FATHER provided the PATTERN for the PURPOSE. And Jesus followed that PATTERN without fail. Following Directions are simply **IMITATING SUCCESS PATTERNS.**

Jesus lived and Practiced GOD, like GOD lived Himself. He did not practice GOD within His own vices, perspectives, and mindset. He practiced GOD, as GOD. I cannot emulate my Teacher amid my own fears, vices, and traumas, and achieve the RESULTS promised. **Many of us are yet respecting our own traumas, while desiring the RESULTS of the Masters.** To achieve those RESULTS, I must first deem my trauma and current mindset, as ILLEGAL. I cannot achieve what the Masters achieve, with the heart of a prisoner and slave. I cannot experience those RESULTS with an illegal spirit. MENTORS desire to assist in the transformation of one's core, by introducing them to THE WAYS OF HIGHEST. But, if we practice "HIGHEST WAYS" from a "legal lowliness," we will find ourselves RE-INTERPRETING the Laws to fit the conveniences of our low spaces. Thus, perverting the Instructions.

A HIGH PLACE demands a ROYAL SPIRIT. It deserves a HIGH PRACTICIONER! I must adhere to the HIGHEST LEVEL to Manifest the products of that Level or DIMENSION.

My DIMENSION SKILLS must be Awakened and Activated within the DIMENSIONS I exist from. I cannot exist within the Embassy of the DIMENSION if I am not a CITZEN, or AUTHORITY of that Dimension. And to be an Authority of that DIMENSION, I must MASTER the RULES and EDUCATION of that DIMENSION!

As citizens, we must **"practice the Practices"** of KINGDOM citizens. We are not simply "as God says" we are. We are the PRACTIONERS of His Word! As Practitioners, we daily produce THE RESULTS of the DIVINE WORD. We create daily. We are not striving to do so. **WE ARE DOING SO!**

WE are not garnered "access, absent of RESPONSIBILITY!" Are we desiring to "hack the Systems?" Are we seeking access in order to learn "what we can escape from Practicing?" Are we seeking to figure out how to Manifest the RESULTS without totally adhering the Instructions? Are we trying to see if the RESULTS are requiring more than what is actually required? Do we sense that we are being fooled and obligated to an unnecessary compliance?

IMITATION of the RULES are but a SIMPLE THING, to the MIND that is totally CONVINCED of the RESULTS and the LAWS.

But, if we feel that our "environments of Life" cannot tell the difference between a "knock off" and the "REAL," we may decide to flash the "knock off," and pay the cheaper value of Practice.

It was honorable for Me to learn it, and live it, in front of those who were more masterful than Me, in order for Me to see, if I actually LEARNED! I could not hide from the Exposure.

I may sound like an actual Professional to the ears of an amateur. But I will sound like an amateur to the ears of the Master.

So, if I'm not careful, I will play to the ears of "who I wish to sound like!" But if I desire to be Perfect, I will play to the ears of those who will make Me work even harder!

The Nature of the ENVIRONMENT in which I wish to guide, will also determine the NATURE in which I FOLLOW DIRECTIONS. If I feel like a Master "leading a company that is blind," then I will invest the fullness of my attention in being challenged. Why, they can't see, anyway! Are YOU seeking to gain the advantage over others, in a way to compensate for your lack of courage? Is this the Reason you continually fail in following directions to the Optimum? Are YOU seeking GREATNESS in order to compensate for your Fear of FAITH and BEING? Are YOU seeking to "learn the Secrets of VISION" in order to provide a "recap" of what an ECHO sounds like to 'those who cannot actually SEE?"

CHAPTER 8
Legitimate Usage

**The LEGITIMACY of OUR LEADERSHIP
is determined by the LEGITIMACY in
which we actually FOLLOW DIRECTIONS**.
Our LAWS OF PRACTICE are determined
within the laws of our authentic hearts and
character. We already know that we cannot
afford to leave out an ingredient, and still
experience the full taste of the Product.
No matter how insignificant a certain
ingredient may be to the final outcome,
that "small thing" will take away something
significant from the Optimum Reality!

Maybe, we sense that certain Instructions
are "insignificant" to the Outcome, you
think? Are we yet compartmentalizing
Divine Things with our own logic? Are we
sensing *that "at least I did the majority" of
what is required? And that the "insignificant
part" will have no ruling over the Whole*? Me
personally, can never fully trust anyone
with THIS TYPE of attitude. They are
showing Me that they would be willing to
grant My Life "a less than Perfect" essential
to my Life*. If YOU perceive that YOUR LIFE
is nothing, YOU WILL NEVER EMBRACE
WHAT IS FULLY REQUIRED FOR IT!*

**ALL INSTRUCTIONS and STEPS are
essential to the Optimum Outcome.**

They are not "simple screws" that are left over after putting that table together. Just because we got the table standing without all the screws, does not mean we put it together perfectly. Maybe, the table is good enough for us, yet it's not good enough for the Designer!

Are YOU desiring to experience the OPTIMUM OUTCOME for Your Life? Or, are YOU simply just looking for it to stand up? Are YOU desiring the Ultimate Intentions that the DESIGNER planned for YOU? Or, have YOU simply settled to have a Life that appears to be Normal, "as long as nothing will test it or shake it?"

We usually FOLLOW INSTRUCTIONS accordingly. What we have internally SETTLED FOR, determines the EFFORTS we invest towards the Reality. When I desire MORE, I will gladly PROVIDE ALL OF ME! When I am settled, I WILL NOT PROVIDE more than that Reality is requiring of ME! If I am taught to BE MORE than I AM WILLING TO BE, I WILL NOT PRACTICE ALL THAT WAS INSTRUCTED OF ME. If I am being taught from a DIMENSION that I have NO INTEREST in, I WILL NOT PRACTICE WHERE INTEREST IS ABSENT.

The CHRIST I am designed to BE, determines the same heart as the

CHRIST from whom I share my PATTERN.
I freely DO WHAT I SEE HIM DOING. And
I will not do what my Conveniences are
allowing Me to get away with.

MENTORSHIP PERSPECTIVES FOR STRATEGISTS

To those assigned to certain, creative
Training and Mentoring:

◎1. Be Patient.

◎2. Be sure of where YOU are Assigned.

◎3. You are there to authentically LEARN
and MASTER the craft, and not just "to
remember what the right answer is!"

◎4. Refrain from the temptation to compare
yourself to other students, and what happens
with them. Your timing is not their timing.

◎5. IMPARTATION has no etiquette. It
takes TIME. True Mentors are not into
"taking your money!" They are seriously
investing "more than knowledge" into YOU.
They are seeking to transform the heart that
created your poverty.

◎6. Be committed to the end. Never declare
an ending that the Teacher has not declared.
Never graduate yourself without honor.

7. Yield to the Process. Process is Preparation.

8. Achieve it FIRST before you share it. The Teacher desires to feel competent with your competency.

9. Never become tolerant of "the least" of your efforts. Go for greater. Stop rushing.

10. Pay attention to the Details. Stop skimming through everything. YOU will get from the Assignment, the same degree you invested yourself into it.

11. Everyone will not encourage YOU. Get out of your feelings. You are being matured in Maturity.

12. Don't sabotage the Process.

13. GOD knows when you're ready.

14. Prayer is necessary for your endurance. IMPARTATION is a destiny and trust Anointing, and not the permission to mimic anointing. It's a breaker anointing, and not just the gift to imitate.

15. Learn to Honor. Learn to do Honorable things.

16. Master your ability to Communicate.

Be patient. Honor your Assignment. Allow it to schedule and prioritize your life happenings.

☜17. Trust your Teachers. They know where they're leading and training YOU. They will not give to YOU what they have never received. Many "teach" what they have never achieved. They do not know the way.

☜18. Pay more than the tuition. Pay the Price of the Shift.

☜19. The Certificate alone, does not mean you've learned. Gain the Wisdom, authentically.

☜20. Wisdom is training YOU to be a Master amongst Masters, and not just just a "greater" in a small world. Teachers want to prepare you to be tested and proven, and not prone to fail.

☜21. Transformation ain't nice. The Mentor will challenge YOU to move beyond your comfort level, constantly. BEYOND, is the path to UPGRADE!